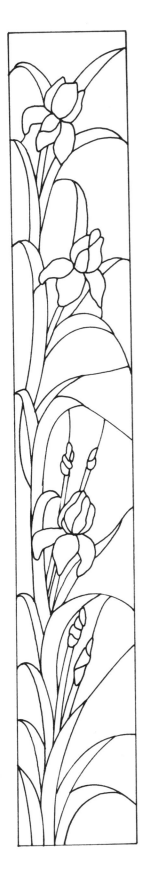
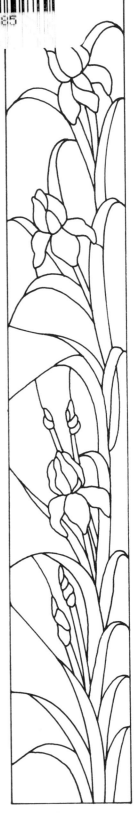

DECORATIVE DOORWAYS STAINED GLASS PATTERN BOOK

151 Designs for Sidelights, Fanlights, Transoms, etc.

CAROLYN RELEI

DOVER PUBLICATIONS, INC.
New York

Copyright © 1990 by Dover Publications, Inc.
All rights reserved under Pan American and International Copyright Conventions.

Published in Canada by General Publishing Company, Ltd., 30 Lesmill Road, Don Mills, Toronto, Ontario.

Decorative Doorways Stained Glass Pattern Book: 151 Designs for Sidelights, Fanlights, Transoms, etc. is a new work, first published by Dover Publications, Inc., in 1990.

DOVER *Pictorial Archive* SERIES

Manufactured in the United States of America
Dover Publications, Inc., 31 East 2nd Street, Mineola, N.Y. 11501

Library of Congress Cataloging-in-Publication Data

Relei, Carolyn
    Decorative doorways stained glass pattern book : 151 designs for sidelights, fanlights, transoms, etc. / Carolyn Relei
          p.   cm.
    ISBN 0-486-26494-7
    1. Glass painting and staining—Patterns.   2. Doorways.
TT298.R45   1990
748.5′022′2—dc20
                                                                    90-38584
                                                                        CIP

PUBLISHER'S NOTE

FOR MANY CENTURIES stained glass has been utilized as a colorful enhancement of architecture. The great cathedrals of Europe present the best-known historical examples of this usage. In the nineteenth century, however, stained glass began to be incorporated more frequently in private residences as the required materials came within the reach of a broader market. The area around doorways was a favored zone for the installation of stained glass windows: to the sides of the door (sidelights), above the door (fanlights and transoms) and on the door itself (rectangles, circles and ovals). This use of stained glass in the home has kept up its appeal and popularity to this day, inspiring the creation of the designs in this book, which can be said to offer a fresh approach to the most enduring features of Victorian stained glass design.

The volume contains 151 designs and, while some are more complicated than others, overall this is a collection of graceful and jewellike stained glass patterns that will delight and challenge even the most accomplished craftspeople. Many themes and motifs are represented here: hummingbirds, morning glories, sea gulls, irises, parrots, herons, roses, tulips, grapes and daffodils. A number of designs are grouped into thematic ensembles for your convenience. Of course, you may find other stained glass applications for these beautiful designs—and you are free to reproduce the patterns in smaller as well as larger sizes.

This collection of patterns is intended as a supplement to stained glass instruction books (such as *Stained Glass Craft* by J. A. F. Divine and G. Blachford, Dover Publications, Inc., 0-486-22812-6). All materials needed, including general instructions and tools for beginners, can usually be purchased from local craft and hobby stores listed in your Yellow Pages.

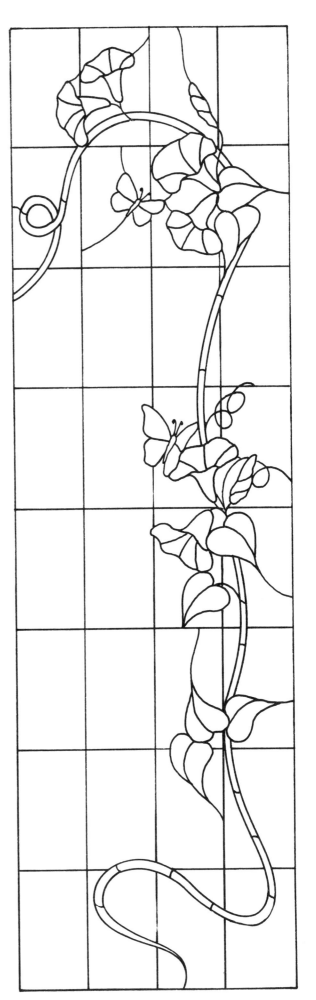

1

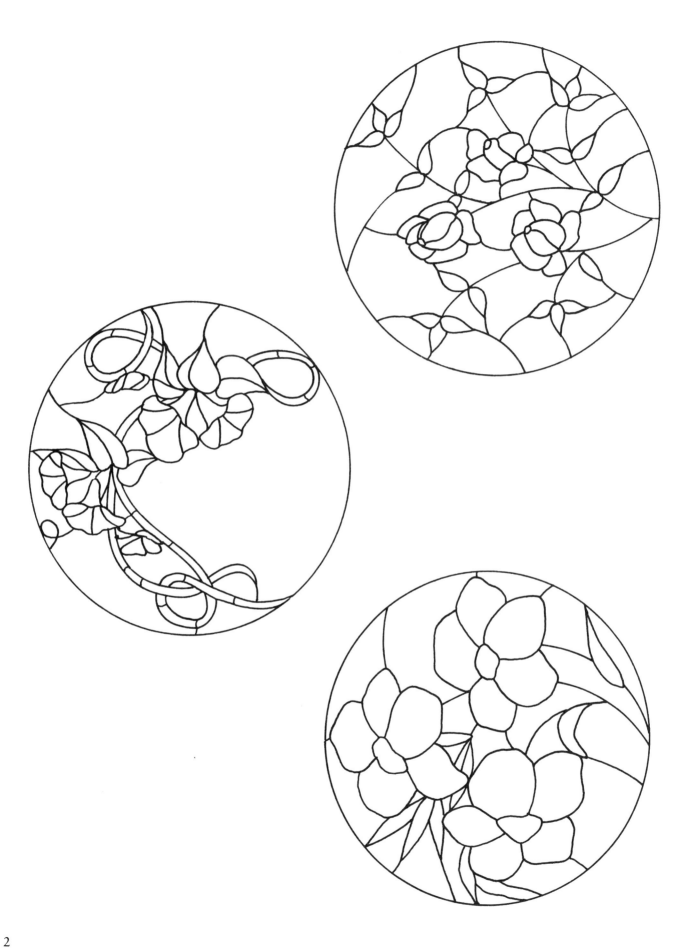

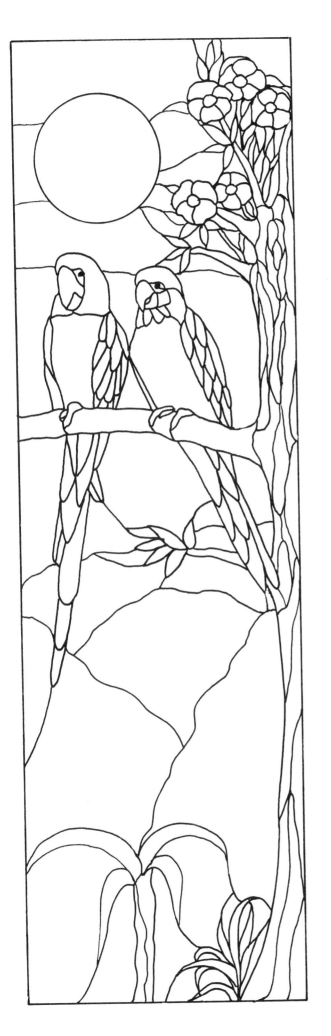 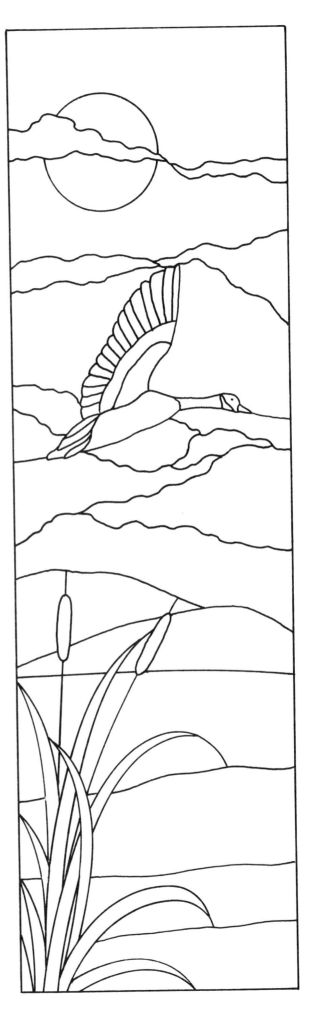

3

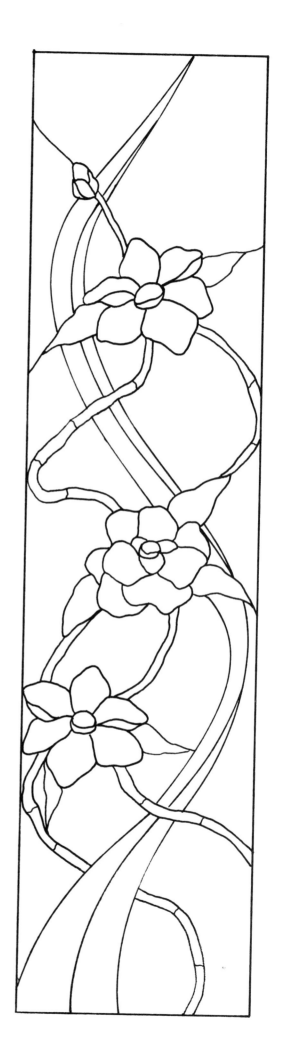

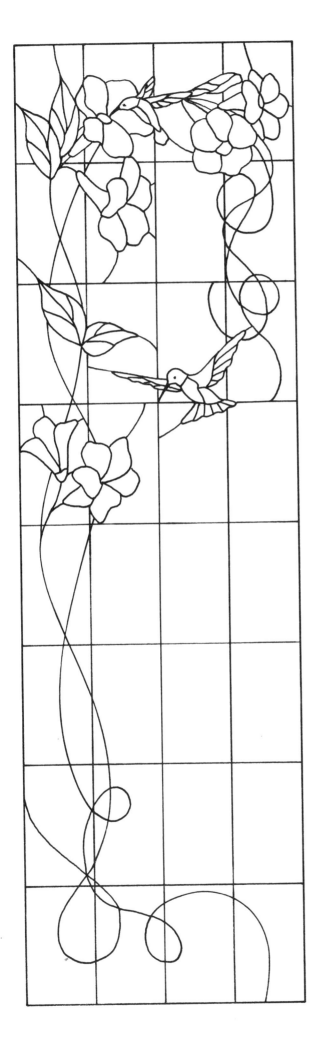
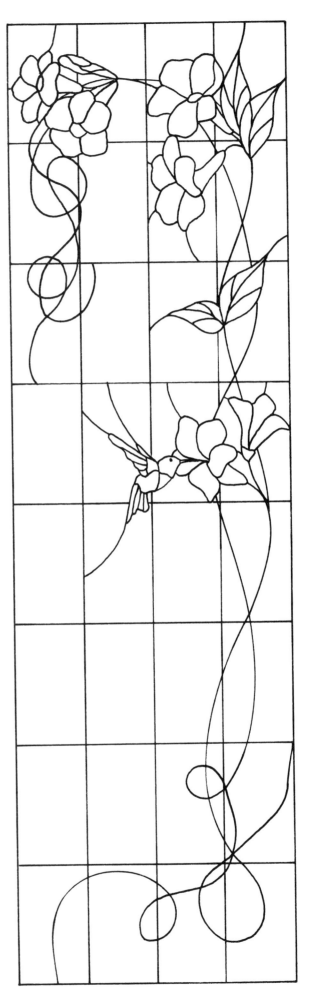

5

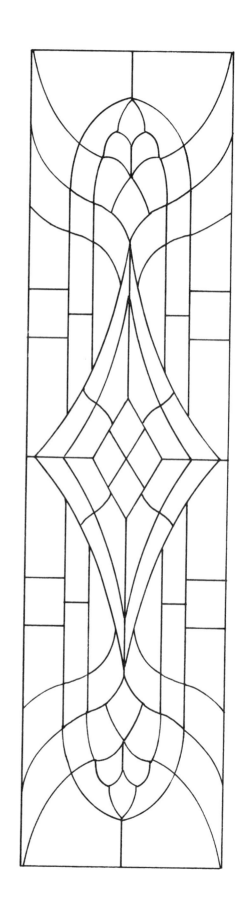

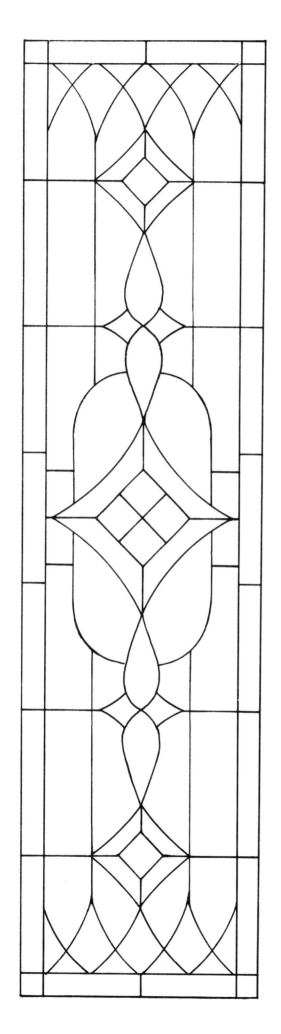

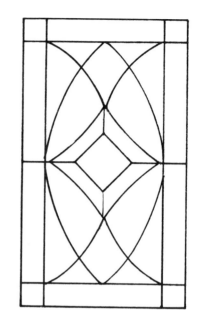

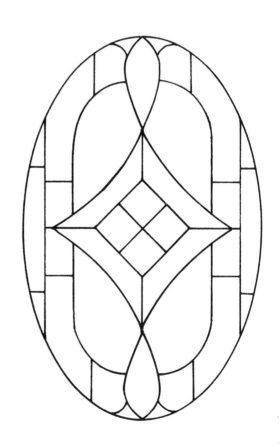

11

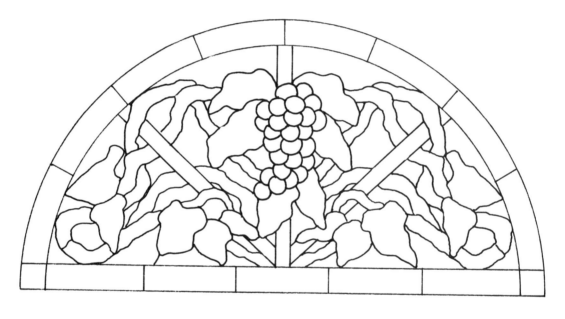

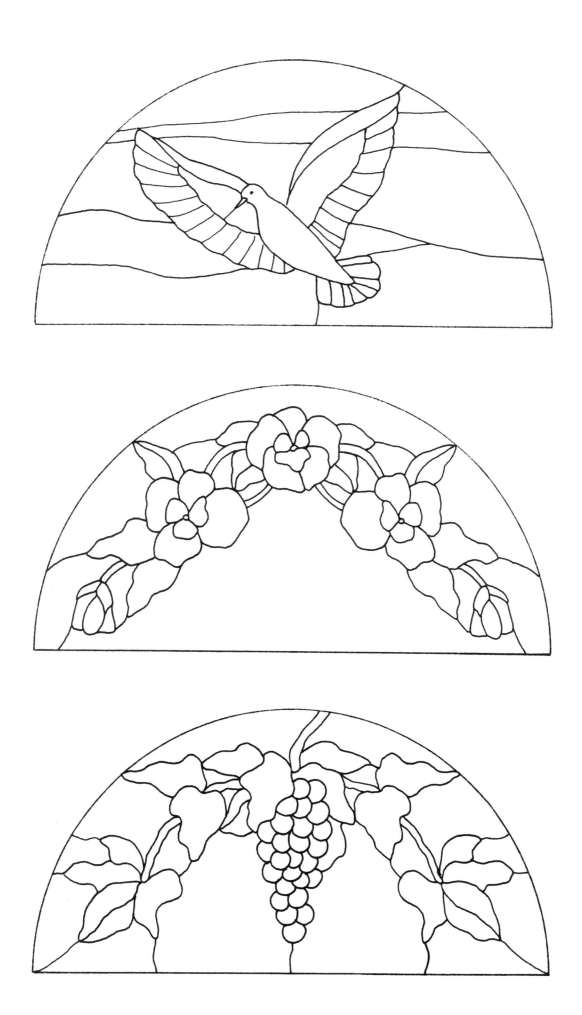

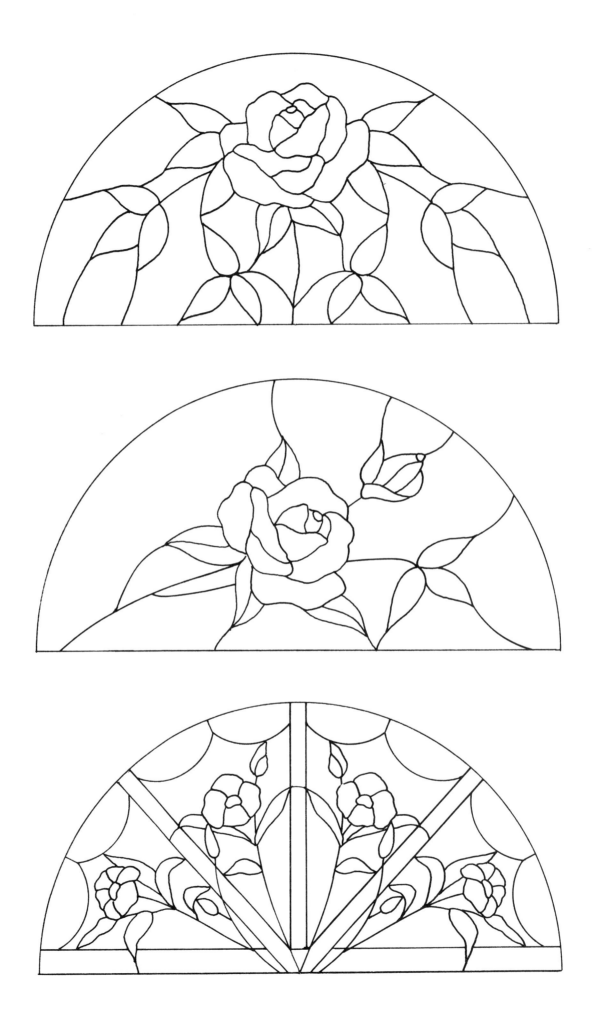

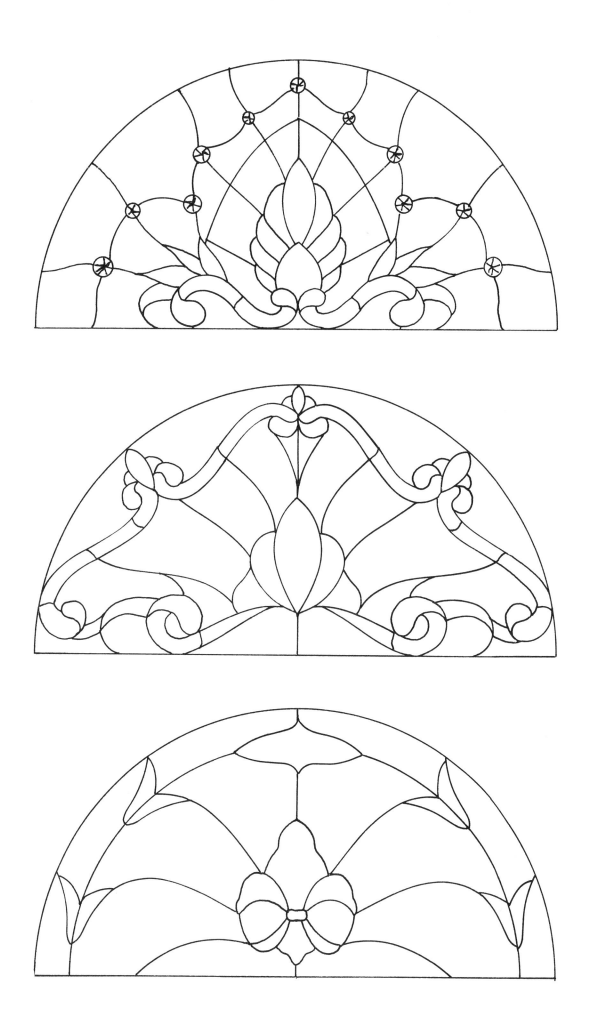

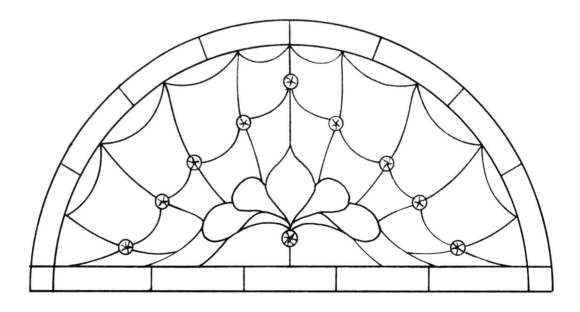

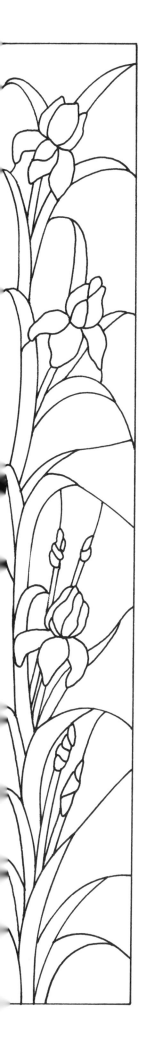

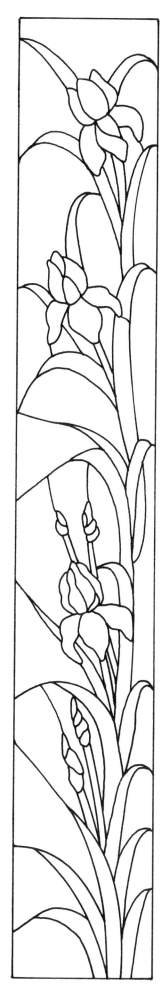

21

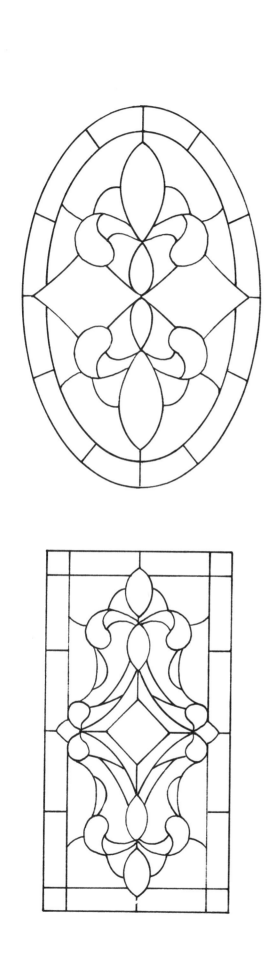
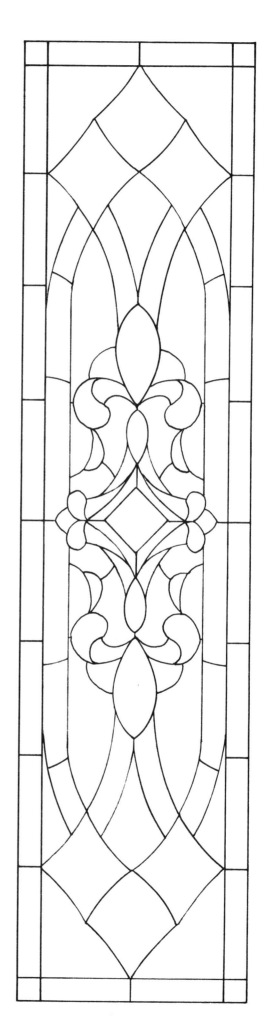

23

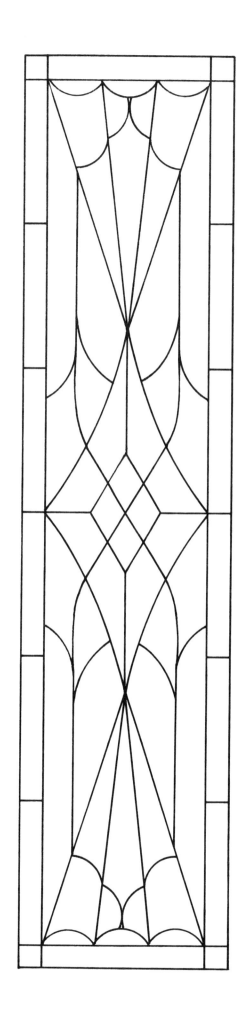
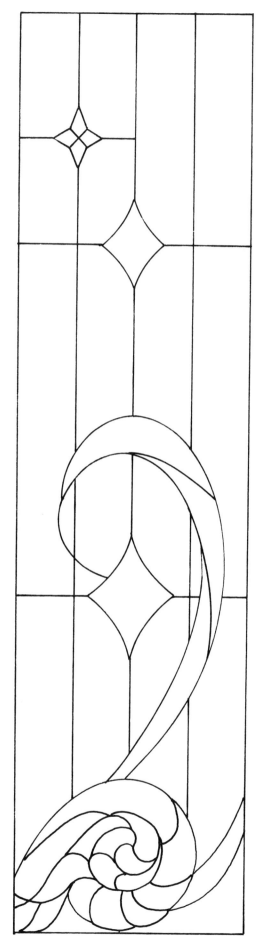

29

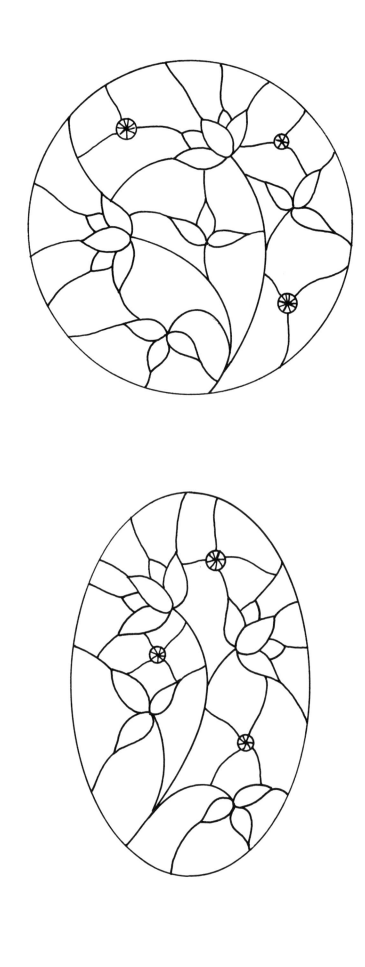

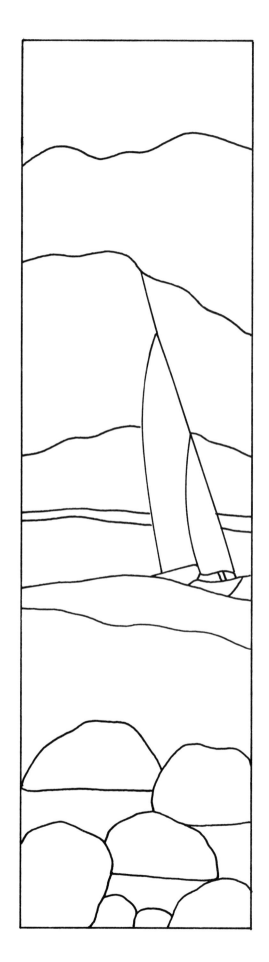

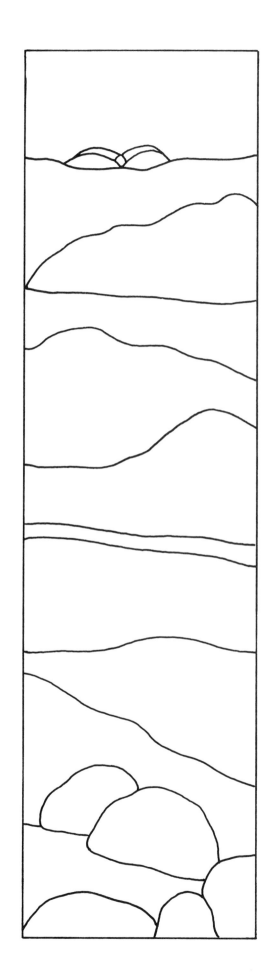

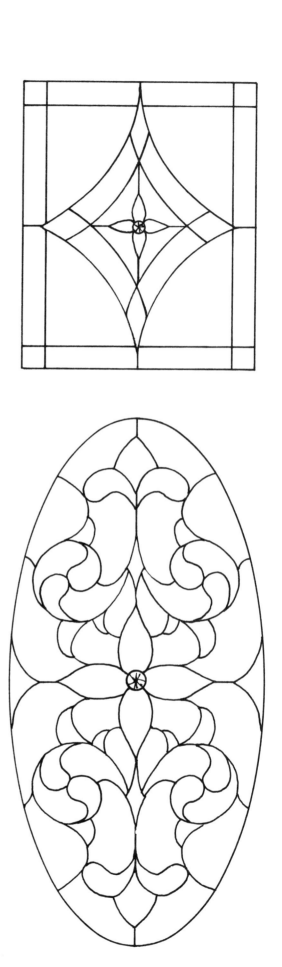

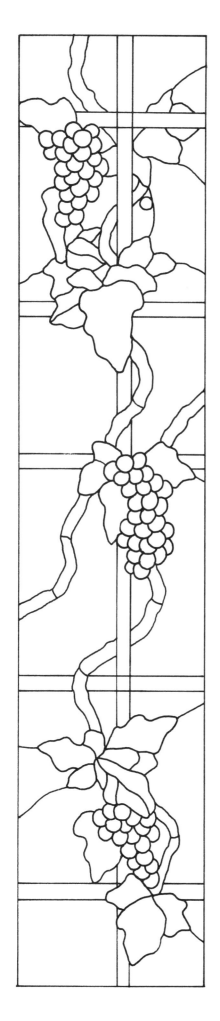

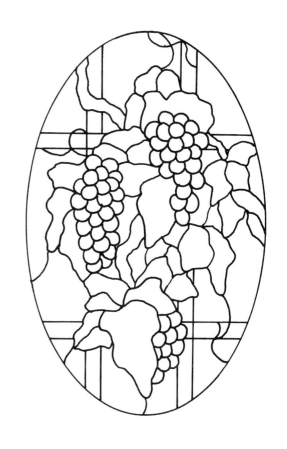

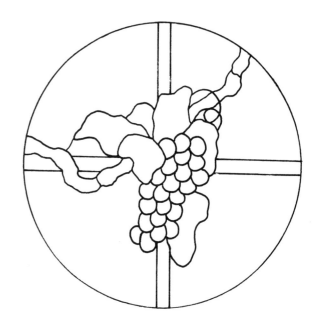

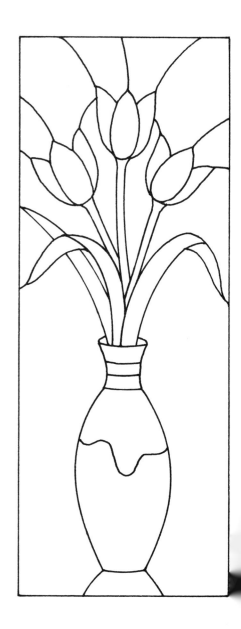

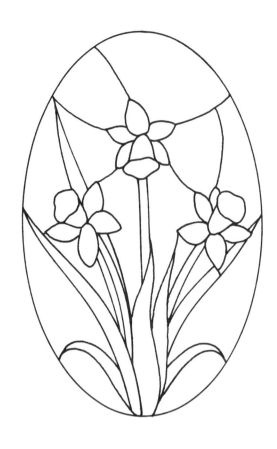

44

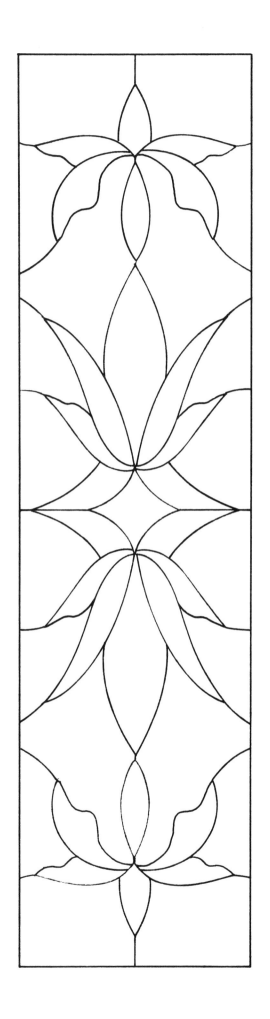

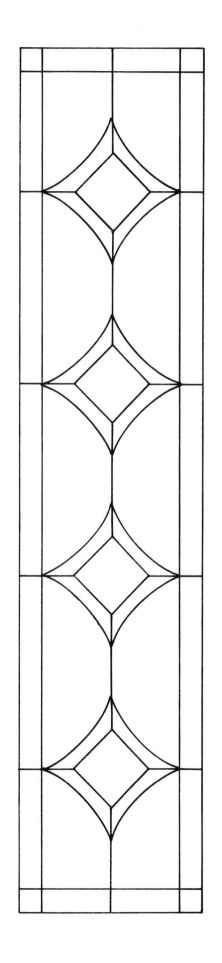

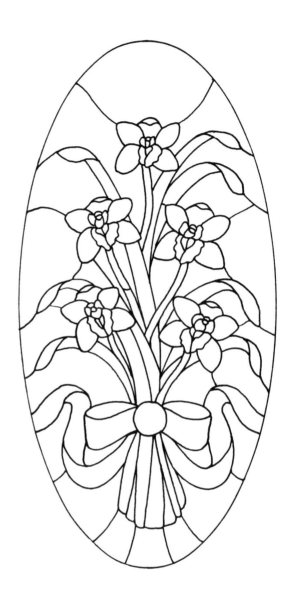

49

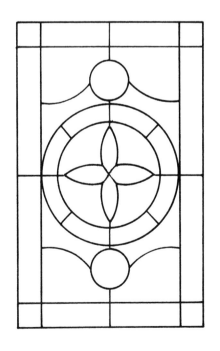

51

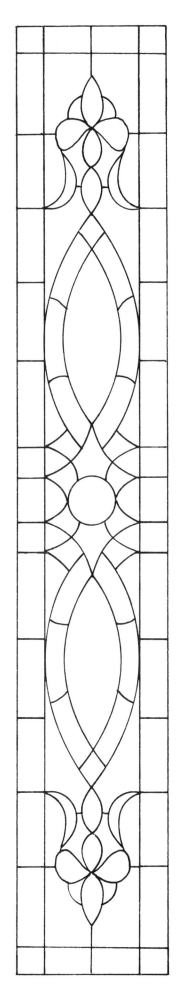

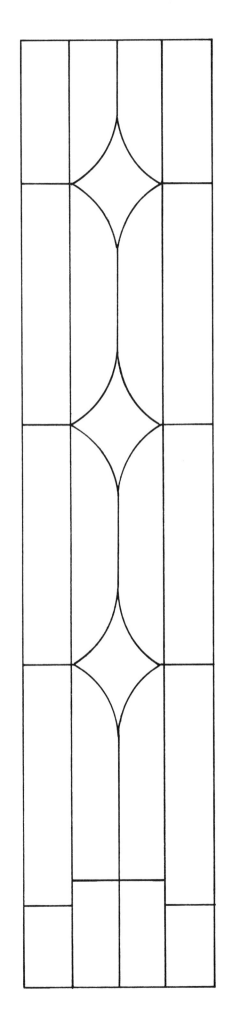

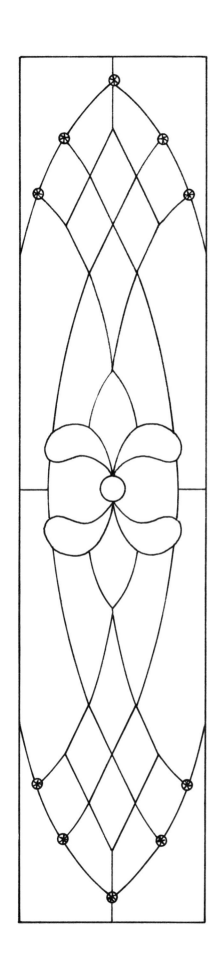

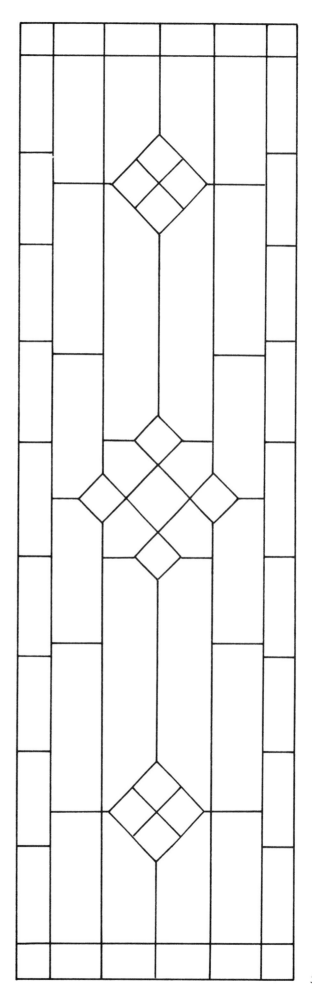

57

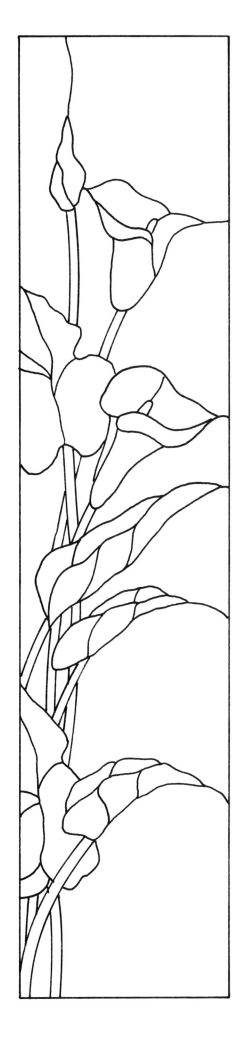
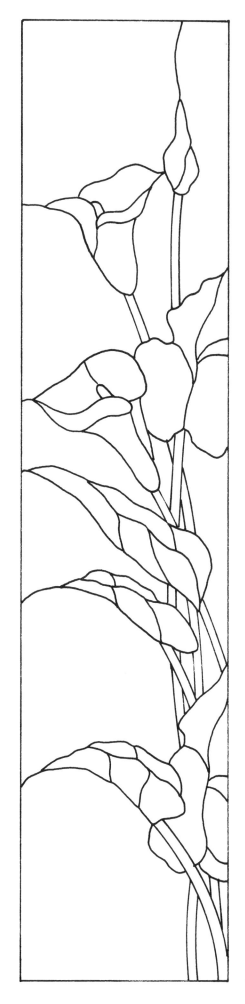

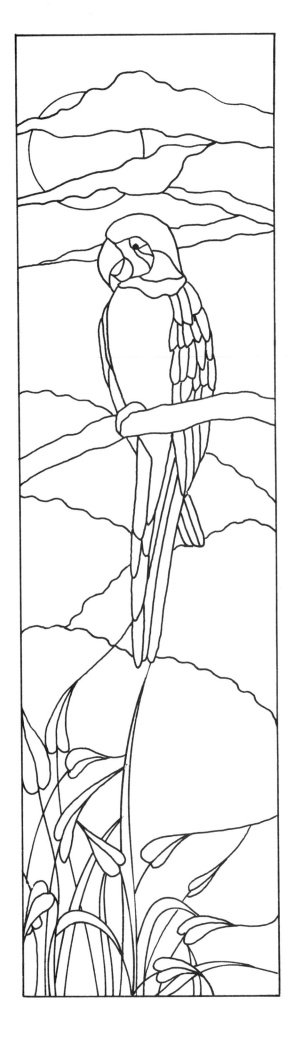